"Green" websites?	2
World Wide Web and the Environment	4
The Greenest Sources of Energy	6
Greening Data Centers	7
Corporate Social Responsibility	9
Green Actions Implemented by Companies and Organizations	11
Earth Hour	13
Sample	15
Research questions	17
Category Environment	17
Use Renewable Sources	17
Black Color	18
Energy Saving Mode	18
Prevent Printing	19
Actions to Protect the Environment	19
Participation in Environmental Events	19
Findings	20
Conclusions	22
Acknowledgments	22
References	23

2013

http://creativecommons.org/licenses/by-nc-nd/3.0/

This work is licensed under a Creative Commons Attribution-NonCommercial-NoDerivs 3.0 Unported License.

"Green" websites?

Websites are "green" when the server that hosts the sites is powered by renewable sources of energy and if it promotes environmental friendly policies (Fire light web studio, 2013; Only websites, 2010). Human beings first meet the green color in nature, in the sight of trees and grass. This is the basic reason why the green color has been combined with nature. Additionally, the green color has been associated with the protection of the environment. The climate change is primarily caused by the greenhouse effect that increases due to human activities and more specifically due to the carbon dioxide (CO_2) (National Oceanic and Atmospheric Administration, 2010). This happens mainly because of the human need to produce more energy so it can be used in services and production (United States Environmental Protection Agency, 2012).

Energy is at the center of the most of critical economical, environmental and developmental issues faces the world. Clean, efficient, affordable and reliable energy is indispensable for global prosperity (The secretary-general's advisory group on energy and climate change, 2010). Nevertheless, protecting the environment, humanity could actually support a healthier future (Brulle & Pellow, 2006; Hayhoe et al., 2004) for their offsprings that will inhabit the planet Earth (McMichael et al., 2003). What is more, it should be mentioned that according to Elizabeth E. Bomberg (1998), another basic reason why the green color is associated with the nature and the environment protection, is the establishment of green political parties. Moreover, it has been associated with art (Endres, Sprain, & Peterson, 2009), communication methods (Milstein, 2012), living (DeLaure, 2011), capitalism, (Singer, 2010), evangelicalism (Lawrence & Terri, 2009) and of course computing (Geronimo, Werner, Westphall, Westphall, & Defenti, 2013; Werner, Geronimo, Westphall, Koch, & Freitas, 2011; Werner et al., 2012).

This article discusses the way a newspaper website can become less energy-consuming and friendlier to the environment (green) and at the same time communicates public understanding on environmental issues. This cannot lead only to a decrease of the environmental destruction (Ekstrom & Moser, 2012), at a level where this particular web industry is responsible, but also to the highlight of a new communication way for more "green" websites for the developers and the companies. The study focuses on this industry (Lester & Hutchins, 2012), because newspapers are a big business, both in print and in its multimedia manifestation. At a global level, in 2011 the newspaper publishing industry produced revenue of about 160 billion USA dollars annually (World Association of Newspapers and News Publishers, 2012). For example, the nytimes.com has more than 30 million unique visitors per month (Peters, 2011). The newspaper industry is not only responsible for the destruction of forests (due to paper usage), but also consumes a substantial amount of energy for powering its websites. Furthermore, through the online reading of websites (Ashworth et al., 2011; Hansen, 2011) the users could realize (public understanding) the fierce ecological problem in the planet earth (Brulle, Carmichael, & Jenkins, 2012; Bulkeley, 2000; Lester, 2010). Finally, companies through social responsibility could provide "green" services to their customers.

World Wide Web and the Environment

The Key World Energy Statistics from the International Energy Agency (IEA) contains timely clearly-presented data on the supply, transformation and consumption of all major energy sources (International Energy Agency, 2012). Additionally, the use of the World Wide Web (WWW) has contributed to a global interconnection among users and creation of new consuming needs.

The WWW has grown to 625 million websites in 2012 (Netcraft, 2012). In this context the introduction of mobile phones (and smartphones in particular) along with the rapid adoption of personal computer use has further increased the need for interconnectivity. The use of WWW, in conjunction with these innovative devices, has led to an incredible growth of the Internet in the last fifteen years (United Nations Environment Programme, 2011). That resulted in a substantially increase of power consumption and thus to more emissions in the atmosphere.

Furthermore, governments and political leaders all over the world have realized the importance of finding solutions to the problem of climate change. They have also created different kinds of organizations for the fulfillment of this purpose. For example, the United States of America (USA) government has founded the Environmental Protection Agency (EPA). EPA's mission is to protect the human health and the environment. EPA submitted a plan on September 30, 2010 to the American Congress. The goals of EPA were:

"Taking action on the climate change and improving air quality, protecting USA's waters, cleaning up communities, advancing sustainable development, ensuring the safety of chemicals, preventing pollution and enforcing environmental laws." (United States Environmental Protection Agency, 2012).

What is more, according to EPA, households in the United States spend 100 USA dollars per year to empower devices while they are switched off (or are in standby mode). Nationwide, the idle gadgets and appliances suck up 100 billion kilowatt per hour of electricity (Energy Star, 2013). Another action of the American government is the Energy Star, a joint program of the U.S. Environmental Protection Agency and the U.S. Department of Energy which helps people to save money and protect the environment through energy efficient products and practices. As we can see in many of our personal computers, there is an Energy Star utility installed. In 2010 Americans with the help of the Energy Star, saved 18 billion USA dollars in their utility bills and have avoided gas emissions equivalent to 33 million cars (Energy Star, 2013).

The Greenest Sources of Energy

The DeSoto Solar Energy Center in Florida has published many surprisingly new facts about energy in the United States:

"DeSoto saves customers almost 7 billion cubic feet of natural gas, 277.000 barrels of oil and avoids 575,000 tons of greenhouse gases, equivalent to removing more than 4.500 cars from the road every year" (Florida Power & Light Company, 2012).

As it is mentioned, there is a significant over waste of energy that leads to increased spending, which could be avoided as we can also read in the paper under the title: "Wind Energy in US Media: A Comparative State-Level Analysis of a Critical Climate Change Mitigation Technology" (Stephens, Rand, & Melnick, 2009). If this happened, the citizens, the environment of the planet and finally the companies would have accomplished their goals. For instance the, Portuguese government has transformed its electric grid from seventeen percent renewable sources to 45 percent in just five years (as of 2010). In the first half of 2012, renewable sources have provided over 25 percent of Germany's electricity. In a sunny day in May of 2012, Germany set a world record by generating 50 percent of its peak electricity needs, only from solar power (Winston, 2012). It is also underlined, that an increasing number of countries tries to exploit renewable sources of energy. This is attributed to the fact that they want to save money and reduce the produced emissions.

Greening Data Centers

By the spread of the World Wide Web, a "new economy" has appeared. This Internet economy also brought new requirements for power and power systems (Mitchell-Jackson, 2001). To begin with, even the most amateur user of the WWW utilizes email services, social networks and even cloud services, (InfoWorld, 2008) even if he/she does not acknowledge it.

Data centers (or centres) providing all these services consume significant amounts of energy and thus accelerate climate change. Obviously, data centers are a basic part of the WWW chain. This is due to the fact that they provide the physical infrastructure for housing computer equipment, often referred to as information technology (IT) equipment. A data center's main function is to provide guaranteed reliable service, security and connectivity to the rest of the Internet via a high-capacity backbone (Mitchell-Jackson, 2001).

The reader can familiarize himself with the installation of a data warehouse by visiting a relative link (http://www.google.com/about/datacenters/gallery) provided by Google company. According to the company itself:

"Across Google, we're currently using renewable energy to power over 30 percent of our operations. We're committed to use renewable energy, like wind and solar, as much as possible" (Google, 2012).

Also, as it is mentioned in the New York Times website, the digital warehouses use about thirty billion watts of electricity, roughly equivalent to the output of thirty nuclear power plants, according to what industry experts have estimated. In particular, data centres' in the United States account for one-quarter to one-third of that load. The study sampled 20,000 servers in about seventy large data centres that drug companies, military contractors, banks, media companies and government agencies use (Glanz, 2012). More details about the contribution in the power consumption of each part of the IT industry (Cook, 2012).

Greenpeace have researched the environmental problems created by the IT industry. Greenpeace suggests that:

"In the same way that the Internet revolutionized how people exchange information, the IT sector can help transform the energy sector to dramatically increase efficiency and interconnectivity while reducing emissions and energy costs" (Greenpeace, 2013).

It is certain that a serious ecological problem is caused by the extended use of the data centers. These centers are usually owned by multinational companies and have extreme gains from the services that they provide to their users though the internet. Establishing standards and increasing green IT awareness is one of the main targets of this particular research as well as other papers (Trimi & Park, 2012) and also such as green cloud computing approaches (Geronimo et al., 2013; Werner et al., 2011; Werner et al., 2012). At this point, it should be suggested that the owners of these companies should use corporate social responsibility strategies towards the planet Earth (Schultz & Wehmeier, 2010) and consumers.

Corporate Social Responsibility

Data Centers are usually part of multinational companies with a large number of stuff. There are techniques and tools that are able to create a more environmentally friendly "green" WWW mainly through the corporate social responsibility (Schultz & Wehmeier, 2010). The corporate social responsibility strategy and the competitive advantage are important issues for the contemporary discussion on corporations in society when taking into account social and environmental impacts. José Milton de Sousa Filho together with other authors wrote:

"Empirically, it can be seen that social responsibility strategies are associated with the competitive advantages, such as attracting valuable employees as well as enhancing the company's image and reputation" (Filho, Wanderley, Gomez, & Farache, 2010).

An important element of the corporate responsibility is the environmental reporting that explains to the general public, a company's, an organization's or a government's environmental performance, encompassing its impacts and its actions on the environment in order to reduce unpleasant effects on the environment or restore environmental conditions (United Nations Economic and Social Commission for Asia and the Pacific, 2012).

Online company reputation risks are already growing more complex, as new digital platforms–social networks, blogs, virtual realities twitter and RSS–rapidly gain acceptance. No digital eraser exists to wipe out the company missteps. Nowadays, we are witnessing both the positive and the negative features of this new era of transparent corporate behavior and instant communication (Weber Shandwick, 2009).

Wrong decisions and actions that can harm the society and the environment may even ruin a company. An example of an online corporate social responsibility which has totally changed the policy of clothes production is the ZARA company. Greenpeace informed the public about the production practices of ZARA's clothes (http://www.greenpeace.org/international/en/campaigns/toxics/water/detox/zara/). According to a Greenpeace online message:

"ZARA clothing items have been found to contain hazardous chemicals. Some of these chemicals break down to form hormone-disrupting chemicals which can then be released into waterways around the world. Traces of cancer-causing chemicals that are released from dyes were also found" (Greenpeace, 2012).

A petition signed by 339.908 users (that included personal information) to change this policy. As a result, in November 29 2012, ZARA company committed to go toxic-free. It should be also added, that even more people were informed about the company's policy through the social networks, blogs and media around the world.
According to Greenpeace:

"Finally, on November 29, 2012 Zara, the world's largest clothing retailer, today announced a commitment to go toxic-free following nine days of intense public pressure. This win belongs to the fashion-lovers, activists, bloggers and denizens of social media. This is people's power in action.' As a result of the action is that Zara now joins Nike, Adidas, Puma, H&M, M&S, C&A and Li-Ning, who have also committed to Detox" (Greenpeace, 2012).

Finally, online corporate responsibility can alter the strategies that have been decided in order to benefit citizens.

Green Actions Implemented by Companies and Organizations

Worldwide multinational companies employ data centers in order to host their websites. In accordance to the latest developments in the ICTs and particularly in the WWW area, they tend to store all their data on the cloud online. According to Greenpeace, research has been conducted in fourteen of all the leading global IT companies which adopt cloud services (Cook, 2012). On the one hand Apple, Amazon and Microsoft are all rapidly expanding and adopting cloud services without adequate concern for their increasing needs for power consumption, and rely heavily on non-renewable sources of energy. On the other hand, Yahoo and Google continue to lead the sector in prioritizing access to renewable sources of energy. Also, they have become more active in supporting policies to lead to a greater renewable energy investment (Cook, 2012) Google, has provided a guided tour inside one of its data center in order to show its openness to the public opinion.

Furthermore, it should be underlined that Facebook, one of the largest online destinations with over one billion users around the world, has now committed to power its platform with renewable energy. Facebook took the first major step in that direction with the construction of its latest data center in Sweden which can be fully powered by renewable energy (Cook, 2012).

Finally, according to the same research, there are indications that a growing number of IT companies are now interested in the environment and tend to use renewable sources of energy. Another study with climate response of the world's 30 largest corporations (Ihlen, 2009) underlines the significance of studying the corporate rhetoric on subjects, such as climate change because it has the power to influence public attention and understanding on this issues. It is worth noting that social responsibility is not limited only to multinational companies. Universities (Rice et al., 2012), where thousands of students study, are also trying to produce fewer emissions. In this way, they are ecologically friendly and will eventually help to deal with the climate change phenomenon.

The MIT University is operating a Campus Energy initiative that has as primary goal to reduce economically energy consumption and associate greenhouse gas emissions (Massachusetts Institute of Technology, 2012). Additionally, the Aristotle University of Thessaloniki (AUTH) that is located in Greece, is implementing actions for the protection of the environment and the reduction of emissions, in a really difficult economical period for Greece (Stamouli & Bouras, 2012). AUTH has about 70.000 students so its aim is to use renewable sources of energy effectively in order meet the need of energy in its facilities (Eco AUTH, 2012).

Earth Hour

The scientific publications concerning climate change as well as the obvious climate changes that are manifasted in various parts of the world, in the form of extreme weather events, have obligated corporations and countries to organize and take part in actions supporting the protection of the environment. On the one hand, the aim of these events is for citizens to realize and take actions for (Lassen, Horsbøl, Bonnen, & Pedersen, 2011) the climate change phenomenon and on the other hand, for corporations to publicly aknowledge the existence of this problem.

A global event (Brulle, 2010) that has started in 2007 is the Earth hour event. The reason why this specific event is mentioned, although there are other similar events too, is that it was mainly started from companies that intended to show social sensitivity (City of Sydney, 2007). It is an event that is really well-known all over the world. In 2012 over a billion people turned off their lights for the Earth hour event, on a Saturday night, in 150 nations around the world. Earth hour's executive director, Andy Ridley, claimed:

> "It's been five years since the first Earth hour in 2007, and the extraordinary growth this year shows hope for action for the planet is not diminishing - instead it's growing" (Cubby, 2012).

The Earth hour (frames the enviroment) (Olausson, 2009) does not only affect citizens and public buildings but also the graphic design of the websites. By this way, websites promote an enviromental friendly message (Lakoff, 2010; Nerlich, Koteyko, & Brown, 2010) to their visitors and thus promote this initiative. In addition, Earth hour dominated social media in 2012, with a video about the event with many views on YouTube at the weekend that the event took place as well as with the graphic design of the website.

What is more, the impact that Earth hour had on social networks was huge. On Twitter, "Earth hour" was among the most popular terms used in English, at the weekend of the event in 2012 (Greenpeace, 2013). The former South African president Nelson Mandela, a celebrity (Anderson, 2011; Lester, 2006) posted the most popular tweet under the Earth hour hashtag. He said: "Let us stand together to make of our world a sustainable source for our future as humanity on this planet" (Earth Hour, 2012). The Facebook website was also used by citizens in war-torn Libya, Kurdistan and northern Iraq to co-ordinate a series of Earth hour events (Earth Hour, 2012). A plug-in was created for Wordpress (a widely used content management system that supports websites) that gives the option to the administrator to redesign the graphic design of his website so it could participate in the Earth hour event (BraveNewCode, 2013).

At this point, it should be underlined that the use of black color in the websites is not a random choice. The use of black color in the graphic design of the websites consumes less energy so it is considered to be friendly to the environment (Roberson et al., 2012). Thus, although green color has been associated with the protection of the environment, black is the color that actually results in less power consumption when employed in websites' graphic design (Heap Media, 2012).

Sample

In order to contribute to the ongoing research regarding the way WWW and online reputation of companies could help in alleviating this problem, the paper in question studies possible methods that can be applied to websites for the protection of the environment and investigates whether such methods are currently implemented in newspaper websites. The research will focus on fifteen newspaper websites from various counties.

The research is based on experiential observation and listing of data collected by researchers, on the selected sample. The scale of evaluation in every question was of dichotomous nature (Yes or No). The research was conducted from 01-11-2012 until 13-11-2012 and the browser employed was Google Chrome. The sample included 15 websites from fifteen counties that exhibit the highest traffic according to Alexa.com and Google rank. The selection of the countries was based on data showing climate change effects from 2007 to 2009 provided by United Nations (Science Compendium, 2009). The fifteen countries that were included in the research were: Australia, Brazil, Canada, China, Germany, Greece, India, the Netherlands, New Zealand, Russian, South Africa, Spain, Turkey, the United Kingdom, and the United States of America. The websites of the sample were: Smh.com.au, folha.uol.com.br, theglobeandmail.com, bild.de, protothema.gr, telegraaf.nl, indiatimes.com, stuff.co.nz, xinhuanet.com, rbc.ru, news24.com, marca.com, hurriyet.com.tr, dailymail.co.uk, global.nytimes.com.

The study attempted to answer the following questions: i) If there is a category about the environment in the websites so that the users can be informed upon the latest matters on this subject, ii) if the servers are powered by renewable sources of energy, (Cook, 2012; Think Host, 2012) iii) if the graphic design of the websites is ecologically friendly, (Heap Media, 2012; Roberson, 2012) iv) if they have an energy saving mode, (Environmental Paper Network, 2007) v) if they prevent printing of articles that are included in the site (Environmental Paper Network, 2007; WWF, 2012) and finally, vi) if the company is interdependent to, or participates in actions that are related to the protection of the environment (CO_2 neutral website, 2012).

When the research was conducted, emails were sent to the newspapers that included queries for additional information. This happened in order to crosscheck the results from the content analysis. Unfortunately, there was only one reply from Fairfax Media (Co-founder of Earth hour).

Research questions

Category Environment

The first question investigated whether the websites under study have a category of articles about the environment so that their readers can be informed about the latest matters on this field (Hansen, 1991). As a primary aim the media should have to inform (Takahashi & Meisner, 2012) but also to (connect) (Olausson, 2011) sensitize their audience through their websites about environmental issues (Berglez, 2011). Media reporting on environmental issues can set a new agenda for the public opinion all over the world (Anderson, 2002). Symbolic politics of media are conducted through articles raising the public's environmental awareness and also influence them (Lester & Hutchins, 2012).

Use Renewable Sources

The second question examined if the servers are powered by renewable sources of energy and if this is mentioned in the website of the newspaper. As it was mentioned above, of data centres are supplied from renewable sources of energy (Geronimo et al., 2013; Stephens et al., 2009; Werner et al., 2011; Werner et al., 2012) and especially when they host websites with millions of visitors, can be a way for reducing the climate change phenomenon. A company that offers real "green" web hosting advertises that:

"Our company commitment to the environment and efforts to minimize negative impact our web hosting business makes on planet Earth very seriously" (Think Host, 2012).

There are also organizations that give certificates for CO2 neutral websites, such as co2neutralwebsite.com. This particular organization states:

"Websites emit carbon due to electricity consumption. Websites can help back the climate through carbon reducing projects. 2,500 websites from 50 countries have joined. Let your website go "green" and receive icon and certificate to put on your website. It will help the Planet earth and further strengthen the brand of your website" (CO2 neutral website, 2012).

Black Color

Another question that was under investigation is whether the websites employ black color as the dominant color in their graphic design or offer their visitors the option to employ black color in the website's graphic design. This can lead to a reduction of power consumption since a substantial number of users visit the newspaper websites. Furthermore, the use of external search engines in the websites of newspapers, such as http://www.blackle.com/, can save more electrical energy through the use of black color (Heap Media, 2012; Roberson, 2012).

Energy Saving Mode

The present study also examined if a black color energy saving mode in the websites of newspapers when the user is inactive. An example of this method is http://www.onlineleaf.com/. More precisely, a plug-in is installed in the website that automatically activates a dark screen when the visitors of the website are inactive. This results in darkening the colors and hiding animations and effects. Consequently, the visitor's monitor does not waste energy (Online Leaf, 2010).

None of the newspaper website was found to use a black color energy saving mode. Provided that newspaper websites with millions of visitors use this kind of mode, a great saving of money and energy will be achieved.

Prevent Printing

The prevention of article printing was also examined in the paper in question. Instead of printing the user can share the article with other users with the help of social networks. Also, the use of WWF documents (see http://www.saveaswwf.com/en) could be employed in order to prevent printing (WWF, 2012).

Actions to Protect the Environment

Another question was, if the newspapers included in the study are interdependent to, or participate in actions that are related to the protection of the environment (International Energy Agency, 2012). The newspaper companies can participate in recycling actions or can finance several groups that protect the environment and publicize it in their websites. Through this, action media companies sensitize and inform their readers about the environment (Olausson, 2011). This could be a new research agenda (Anderson, 2009) for the most pressing issue of our time.

Participation in Environmental Events

Finally, it was investigated (by sending emails) if newspaper websites have (communication) participated in environmental actions (Norton, 2007) in any way (not simply by publishing an article about it) in events like Earth hour or other citizen participation events (Lassen et al., 2011), that protect the environment. The only newspaper website answered this question was smh.com.au it sent a picture in which it was shown that it has changed its background page for the Earth hour.

Findings

Table 1. includes the results from the questions presented in detail in the previous section. The results of the study is be presented and discussed below.

Countries	Websites	Questions						
		Category Environment	Use renewable sources	Black colour	Energy saving mode	Prevent printing	Actions Protect the environment	Website participate
Australia	smh.com.au	YES	NO	NO	NO	NO	YES	YES
Brazil	folha.uol.com.br	YES	NO	NO	NO	NO	NO	NO
Canada	Theglobeandmail.com	YES	NO	NO	NO	NO	NO	NO
Germany	bild.de	YES	NO	NO	NO	NO	NO	NO
Hellenic Republic	protothema.gr	YES	NO	NO	NO	NO	NO	NO
Netherlands	telegraaf.nl	NO	NO	NO	NO	NO	NO	NO
India	indiatimes.com	YES	NO	NO	NO	YES	NO	NO
New Zealand	stuff.co.nz	YES	NO	NO	NO	NO	NO	NO
China	xinhuanet.com	YES	NO	NO	NO	NO	NO	NO
Russian	rbc.ru	NO	NO	NO	NO	NO	NO	NO
South Africa	news24.com	YES	NO	NO	NO	NO	NO	NO
Spain	MARCA.com	NO	NO	NO	NO	NO	NO	NO
Turkey	hurriyet.com.tr	NO	NO	NO	NO	NO	NO	NO
United Kingdom	dailymail.co.uk	NO	NO	NO	NO	NO	NO	NO
United States of America	global.nytimes.com	YES	NO	NO	NO	NO	NO	NO
% of positive answers		66.6%	0%	0%	0%	6.6%	6.6%	6.6%

According to the results of the questions examined, 66.6 percent of the newspaper websites has a special category including articles about environmental issues.

In general, it seems that the public opinion gets informed about the environment, and the climate change phenomenon that Planet Earth deals with. It is really reasonable for newspapers to give emphasis on promoting environmental issues (Lester, 2009). Informing the readers is a really important step, in order for everyone to realize and take actions for this serious problem. Additionally, concerning the hosting of newspaper websites examined, none of them was powered by renewable sources of energy. There was no sign or logo in any of the websites indicating that they are powered in such a way.

The companies that are actually interested in the environment and have a social company responsibility strategy have a marketing opportunity (Hansen & Machin, 2008) to power their websites with renewable sources of energy. Furthermore, they will improve their brand image to their customers with future benefits for their corporations. As far as graphic design of the websites is concerned, newspaper websites may include the option of displaying their content mainly in black color. This was not found in any of the websites that were researched. The users should decide whether they prefer black color to the website they visit which consumes less energy.

Furthermore, a black color saving mode in the websites could be shown up on the screen when the user is inactive, a feature that was not offered by any of the websites under study.

Another solution in order for a website to consider "green" is by not allowing readers to print the articles. However, only one website did not allow the users to print its content. In this way, they contribute to the protection of the environment because fewer trees are going to be cut down for printing purposes.

The companies that actually want to show social responsibility have to be active in movements (actions) that protect the environment. They could also promote such actions to their readers in order for them to be informed. There are organizations that provide trademarks (logos) indicating that company websites are taking actions to protect the environment. Such logos were not used in the sample of this research.

Finally, one of the questions of the research was whether the newspaper websites protect the environment by making changes in their websites during events that focus on environmental protection issues such as Earth hour event. Only one company changed the appearance of its website during the Earth hour event. The change in the wallpaper of the website shows that the website participates in "green" actions. In this way, this particular action communicates people the message to save energy so that a greener planet can be achieved.

Conclusions

To begin with, the problem of the climate change is constantly intensified and unfortunately its results are obvious in all over the world. Nations, organizations and companies should take immediate environmental decisions and take actions. The use of renewable sources of energy is one of the ways that nations can follow in order to protect the environment.

The website industry and specifically data centers are a new rising economy with multiple gains which can influence millions of users. This industry consumes and maybe wastes huge amounts of energy for its operation. The findings of this research indicate that the creation of "green" newspaper websites saving energy and sensitizing users about the environment is in the initial stage of development. It has been concluded that the majority of the media companies researched in the present paper did not take any actions for environmental protection and against global warming effect. What is more the paper underlines the significance of using particular characteristics and tools in company websites so that they communicate "green" thinking to the public in order to become less energy-consuming.

Acknowledgments

We would like to thank Pavlos A. Stamatopoulos for the cover.

References

Anderson, A. (2002). The Media Politics of Oil Spills. *Spill Science & Technology Bulletin*, 7(5), 7-16.

Anderson, A. (2009). Media, Politics and Climate Change: Towards a New Research Agenda. *Sociology Compass*, 3(2), 166-182.

Anderson, A. (2011). Sources, media, and modes of climate change communication: the role of celebrities. *WIREs Climate Change*, 2(4), 535-546.

Ashworth, P., Jeanneret, T., Gardner, J., & Shaw, H. (2011). *Communication and climate change: What the Australian public thinks*. Retrieved from http://www.csiro.au/files/files/p11fh.pdf

BraveNewCode. (2013). *Earth Hour*. Retrieved from http://wordpress.org/extend/plugins/earth-hour/screenshots/

Berglez, P. (2011). Inside, outside, and beyond media logic: journalistic creativity in climate reporting. *Media, Culture and Society*, 33(3), 449-465.

Bomberg, E. (1998). *Green Parties and Politics in the European Union*. London: Routlenge.

Brulle, R. J., & Pellow, D. N. (2006). Environmental justice: Human Health and Environmental Inequalities. *Annu. Rev. Public Health*, 27, 103-124.

Brulle, R. J. (2010). From Environmental Campaigns to Advancing the Public Dialog: Environmental Communication for Civic Engagement. *Environmental Communication: A Journal of Nature and Culture*, 4(1), 82- 98.

Brulle, R., Carmichael, J., & Jenkins, C. (2012). Shifting public opinion on climate change: an empirical assessment of factors influencing concern over climate change in the U.S., 2002-2010. *Climatic Change*, 114(2), 169-188.

Bulkeley, H. (2000). Common knowledge? Public understanding of climate change in Newcastle, Australia. *Public Understand. Sci.,* 9, 313-334.

City of Sydney. (2007). *Earth Hour-Earth Always*. Retrieved from http://www.sydneymedia.com.au/3263-earth-hour-earth-always/

Cook, G. (2012). *How Clean is Your Cloud?*. Retrieved from http://www.greenpeace.org/international/Global/international/publications/climate/2012/iCoal/HowCleanisYourCloud.pdf

CO2 neutral website. (2012). *CO2 neutral website*. Retrieved from http://www.co2neutralwebsite.com

Cubby, Ben. (2012). *One-night stand: more than a billion switch off*. Retrieved from http://www.smh.com.au/environment/earth-hour/onenight-stand-more-than-a-billion-switch-off-20120401-1w6m9.html

DeLaure, M. (2011). Environmental Comedy: No Impact Man and the Performance of Green Identity. *Environmental Communication: A Journal of Nature and Culture*, 5(4), 447-466.

Earth Hour. (2012). *History*. Retrieved from http://www.wwf.org.au/earthhour/history/

Eco AUTH. (2012). *Eco AUTH*. Retrieved from http://eco.auth.gr/wordpress/?page_id=349

Ekstrom, J. A., & Moser, S. C. (2012). *Climate Change Impacts, Vulnerabilities, and Adaptation in the San Francisco Bay Area: A Synthesis of PIER Program Reports and Other Relevant Research (CEC-500-2012-071)*. PIER report for the California Energy Commission. Retrieved from http://www.energy.ca.gov/2012publications/CEC-500-2012-071/CEC-500-2012-071.pdf

Endres, D., Sprain, L., & Peterson, R. (2009). *Social Movement to Address Climate Change: Local Steps for Global Action*. Amherst, NY: Cambria Press.

Energy Star. (2013). *Standby Power and Energy Vampires*. Retrieved from http://www.energystar.gov/index.cfm?c=about.vampires

Energy Star. (2013). *About Energy Star*. Retrieved from http://www.energystar.gov/index.cfm?c=about.ab_index

Environmental Paper Network. (2007). *The State of the Paper Industry*. Retrieved from http://www.greenpressinitiative.org/documents/StateOfPaperInd.pdf

Filho, J. M. de S., Wanderley, L. S. O., Gomez, C. P., & Farache, F. (2010). Strategic corporate social responsibility management for competitive advantage, BAR. *Brazilian Administration Review*, 7(3), 294-309.

Fire light web studio. (2013). *Eco-Friendly "Green" Websites*. Retrieved from http://www.firelightwebstudio.com/index.php?option=com_content&view=article&id=98&Itemid=120

Florida Power & Light Company. (2012). *Clean Energy for the Next Generation*. Retrieved from http://www.fpl.com/environment/solar/pdf/Desoto.pdf

Geronimo, G.A., Werner, J., Westphall, C.B., Westphall, C. M., & Defenti L. (2013 January - February). Provisioning and Resource Allocation for Green Clouds. *ICN 2013: The Twelfth International Conference on Networks*, Seville, Spain.

Glanz, J. (2012). *The cloud factories*. Retrieved from http://www.nytimes.com/2012/09/23/technology/data-centers-waste-vast-amounts-of-energy-belying-industry-image.html?_r=2&

Google. (2012). *Inside our data centers*. Retrieved from http://www.google.com/about/datacenters

Greenpeace. (2012). *No More Fashion Victims*. Retrieved from http://www.greenpeace.org/international/en/campaigns/toxics/water/detox/zara/

Greenpeace. (2012). *People! Zara commits to go toxic-free*. Retrieved from http://www.greenpeace.org/international/en/news/features/Zara-commits-to-go-toxic-free/

Greenpeace. (2013). *IT-enabled climate solutions*. Retrieved from http://www.greenpeace.org/international/en/campaigns/climate-change/Climate-negotiations-in-Cancun/climate-change/cool-it/Solutions/

Heap Media. (2012). *How is Blackle saving energy?*. Retrieved from http://www.blackle.com/about/

Hansen, A. (1991). The media and social construction of the enviroment. *Media, Culture and Society*, 13, 443-458.

Hansen, A., & Machin, D. (2008). Visually branding the environment: climate change as a marketing opportunity. *Discourse Studies*, 10(6), 777-794.

Hansen, A. (2011). Communication, media and environment: Towards reconnecting research on the production, content and social implications of environmental communication. *International Communication Gazette*, 73(1-2), 7-25.

Hayhoe, K., Cayan, D., Field, B. C., Frumhoff, P. C., Maurer, E. P., Miller, N. L., … Verville, J. H. (2004). Emissions pathways, climate change, and impacts on California. *Proc. Natl. Ac. Sc*, 101(34), 12422-12427.

Ihlen, Ø. (2009). Business and Climate Change: The Climate Response of the World's 30 Largest Corporations. *Environmental Communication: A Journal of Nature and Culture*, 3(2), 244-262.

InfoWorld. (2008). *What cloud computing really means*. Retrieved from http://www.infoworld.com/d/cloud-computing/what-cloud-computing-really-means-031

International Energy Agency. (2012). *C02 Emissions from fuel combustion*. Retrieved from http://www.iea.org/publications/freepublications/publication/CO2emissionfromfuelcombustionHIGHLIGHTS.pdf

International Energy Agency. (2012). *Key World Energy Statistics*. Retrieved from http://www.iea.org/publications/freepublications/publication/kwes.pdf

Lassen, I., Horsbøl, A., Bonnen, K., & Pedersen, A. (2011). Climate Change Discourses and Citizen Participation: A Case Study of the Discursive Construction of Citizenship in Two Public Events. *Environmental Communication: A Journal of Nature and Culture*, 5(4), 411-427.

Lakoff, G. (2010). Why it Matters How We Frame the Environment. *Environmental Communication: A Journal of Nature and Culture*, 4(1), 70-81.

Lawrence, J. P., & Terri, S. W. (2009). Rhetorical Features of Green Evangelicalism. *Environmental Communication: A Journal of Nature and Culture*, 3(2), 224-243.

Lester, L. (2006). Lost in the Wilderness? Celebrity, Protest and the News. *Journalism Studies,* 7(6), 907-921.

Lester, L., & Hutchins B. (2009). Power games: environmental protest, news media and the internet. *Media, Culture and Society*, 31(4), 579-594.

Lester, L. (2010). Big tree, small news: Media access, symbolic power and strategic intervention. *Journalism*, 11(5), 589-606.

Lester, L., & Hutchins, B. (2012). Soft journalism, politics and environmental risk: An Australian story. *Journalism*, 13(5), 654-667.

Lester, L., & Hutchins, B. (2012). The power of the unseen: environmental conflict, the media and invisibility. *Media, Culture and Society*, 34(7), 847-863.

Lester, L., & Hutchins, B. (2012). Journalism, the environment and the new media politics of invisibility. *Australian Journalism Review*, 34(2), 19-31.

Massachusetts Institute of Technology. (2012). *Campus Energy*. Retrieved from http://mitei.mit.edu/campus-energy

McMichael, A. J., Campbell-Lendrum, D. H., Corvalán, C. F., Ebi, K. L., Githeko, A. K., Scheraga, J. D., & Woodward, A. (2003). *Climate change and human health*. Retrieved from http://www.who.int/globalchange/publications/climchange.pdf

Milstein, T. (2012). Greening Communication. In S.D. Fassbinder, A. J. Nocella II. & R. Kahn (Eds.), *Greening the Academy: Ecopedagogy through the Liberal Arts* (pp. 161-174). Rotterdam: Sense Publishers.

Mitchell-Jackson, J. (2001). Energy Needs in an Internet Economy: A Closer Look at Data Centers. University of California, Berkeley.

National Oceanic and Atmospheric Administration. (2010). *Greenhouse Gases Frequently Asked Questions*. Retrived from http://www.ncdc.noaa.gov/oa/climate/gases.html

Nerlich, B., Koteyko, N., & Brown, B. (2010). Theory and language of climate change communication. *WIREs Clim Change*, 1(1), 97-110.

Netcraft. (2012). *November 2012 Web Server Survey*. Retrieved from http://news.netcraft.com/archives/2012/11/01/november-2012-web-server-survey.html

Norton, T. (2007). The Structuration of Public Participation: Organizing Environmental Control. *Environmental Communication: A Journal of Nature and Culture*, 1(2), 146-170.

Olausson, U. (2009). Global warming-global responsibility? Media frames of collective action and scientific certainty. *Public Understanding of Science*, 18(4), 421-436.

Olausson, U. (2011). "We're the Ones to Blame": Citizens' Representations of Climate Change and the Role of the Media. *Environmental Communication: A Journal of Nature and Culture*, 5(3), 281-299.

Olausson, U. (2011). Explaining Global Media: A Discourse Approach. In P. Pachura (Ed.), *The Systemic Dimension of Globalization* (pp. 125-138). Croatia: InTech.

Online Leaf. (2010). *Standby for a greener web*. Retrieved from http://www.onlineleaf.com/

Only websites. (2010). *Green Websites*. Retrieved from http://www.onlywebsites.com/green.php

Peters, J. (2011). Times's Online Pay Model Was Years in the Making. Retrieved from http://www.nytimes.com/2011/03/21/business/media/21times.html?pagewanted=1&tntemail1=y&_r=2&emc=tnt

Roberson, J., Homan, G., Mahajan, A., Nordman, B., Webber, C., Brown, R., ... Koomey, J. (2012). *Energy Use and Power Levels in New Monitors and Personal Computers (LBNL-48581)*. Retrieved from http://enduse.lbl.gov/Info/LBNL-48581.pdf

Rice, R. E., Meisner, M., Depoe, S., Opel, A., Roser-Renouf, C., & Shome, D. (2012). Environmental Communication and Media: Centers, Programs and Resources. In S. Jones (Ed.), *Communication @ the Center* (pp.137-155). New York: Hampton Press.

Science Compendium. (2009). *Climate Change*. Retrieved from http://www.unep.org/pdf/ccScienceCompendium2009/cc_ScienceCompendium2009_full_en.pdf

Schultz, F., & Wehmeier, S. (2010). Institutionalization of corporate social responsibility within corporate communications: Combining institutional, sensemaking and communication perspectives. *Corporate Communications: An international Journal*, 15(1), 9-29.

Singer, R. (2010). Neoliberal Style, the American ReGeneration, and Ecological Jeremiad in Thomas Friedman's "Code Green". *Environmental Communication: A Journal of Nature and Culture*, 4(2), 135-151.

Stamouli, N., & Bouras, S. (2012). *Greeks Raid Forests in Search of Wood to Heat Homes*. Retrieved from http://online.wsj.com/article/SB10001424127887324442304578232280995369300.html?KEYWORDS=10000+trees+in+greece

Stephens, J. C., Rand, G. M., & Melnick, L. L. (2009). Wind Energy in US Media: A Comparative State-Level Analysis of a Critical Climate Change Mitigation Technology. *Environmental Communication: A Journal of Nature and Culture*, 3(2), 168-190.

Takahashi, B., & Meisner, M. (2012). Climate change in Peruvian newspapers: The role of foreign voices in a context of vulnerability. *Public Understanding of Science*, 22, 427-442.

The secretary-general's advisory group on energy and climate change. (2010). *Energy for a Sustainable Future*. Retrieved from http://www.un.org/wcm/webdav/site/climatechange/shared/Documents/AGECC%20summary%20report[1].pdf

Think Host. (2012). *Our Mission*. Retrieved from http://www.thinkhost.com/

Trimi, S., & Park, S. (2012). Green IT: practices of leading firms and NGOs. *Service Business*, 1-17.

United Nations Economic and Social Commission for Asia and the Pacific. (2012). *Corporate social responsibility and environmental reporting*. Retrieved from http://www.unescap.org/esd/environment/lcgg/documents/roadmap/case_study_fact_sheets/Fact%20Sheets/FS-Corporate-Social-Responsibility-and-environmental-reporting.pdf

United Nations Environment Programme. (2011). *Keeping Track of Our Changing Environment*. Retrieved from http://www.unep.org/geo/pdfs/keeping_track.pdf

United States Environmental Protection Agency. (2012). *Carbon Dioxide Emissions*. Retrieved from http://www.epa.gov/climatechange/ghgemissions/gases/co2.html

United States Environmental Protection Agency. (2012). *Strategic plan*. Retrieved from http://www.epa.gov/planandbudget/strategicplan.html

Winston, A. (2012). *The Supposed Decline of Green Energy*. Retrieved from http://www.bloomberg.com/news/2012-09-26/the-supposed-decline-of-green-energy.html

Weber Shandwick. (2009). *Reputations online*. Retrieved from http://www.online-reputations.com/DLS/RiskyBusiness_WhitePaper_US.pdf

Werner, J., Geronimo, G.A., Westphall, C.B., Koch F. L., & Freitas, R. (2011). Simulator improvements to validate the Green Cloud Computing approach. *In 7th Latin American Network Operations and Management Symposium*, 1-8.

Werner, J., Geronimo, G. A., Westphall, C. B., Koch, F. L., Freitas, R. R., & Westphall, C. M. (2012). Environment, Services and Network Management for Green Clouds. *CLEI Electronic Journal*, 15(2).

World Association of Newspapers and News Publishers. (2012). *World press trends 2011*. Retrieved from http://www.wan-ifra.org/articles/2012/04/17/world-press-trends-2011

WWF. (2012). *How to save a Tree*. Retrieved from http://www.saveaswwf.com/en/what-is-it.html

www.antonopoulos.info
Antonopoulos Nikos is candidate for PhD degree in the School of Journalism and Mass Communications at the Aristotle University of Thessaloniki. He received his BSc in Information Technology and Telecommunications at the Higher Technological Educational Institute of Larissa, MSc in Cultural Informatics and Communication at the Aegean University. His research interests include online media, human-computer interaction, social networking and web communication.

www.blogs.auth.gr/veglis
Andreas Veglis is Associate Professor, head of the Media Informatics Lab in the School of Journalism and Mass Communications at the Aristotle University of Thessaloniki. He received his BSc in Physics, MSc in Electronics and Communications, and PhD in Computer Science, all from Aristotle University. In November of 2010 he was elected head of the postgraduate programme of the School of Journalism and Mass Communications, Aristotle University of Thessaloniki. In March of 2012 he was elected Deputy Chairman of the Department of Journalism Mass Media Communication. His research interests include information technology in journalism, new media, course support environments, and distance learning. He is the author or co-author of ten books, he has published 50 papers on scientific journals and he has presented 65 papers in international and national Conferences. Dr. Veglis has been involved in 11 national and international research projects.

www.ingramcontent.com/pod-product-compliance
Lightning Source LLC
Chambersburg PA
CBHW081756170526
45167CB00009B/4038